W9-AGM-445

Buses

by Allison Lassieur

Consultant:
Donald M. Coffin, Vice President
Museum of Bus Transportation
Hawley, Pennsylvania

Bridgestone Books
an imprint of Capstone Press
Mankato, Minnesota

Bridgestone Books are published by Capstone Press
818 North Willow Street, Mankato, Minnesota 56001
http://www.capstone-press.com

Copyright © 2000 Capstone Press. All rights reserved.
No part of this book may be reproduced without written permission from the publisher.
The publisher takes no responsibility for the use of any of the materials
or methods described in this book, nor for the products thereof.
Printed in the United States of America.

Library of Congress Cataloging-in-Publication Data
Lassieur, Allison.
    Buses/by Allison Lassieur.
    p. cm.—(The transportation library)
    Includes bibliographical references and index.
    Summary: Discusses the inventors, history, early models, major parts, and workings
of buses.
    ISBN 0-7368-0360-2
    1. Buses—Juvenile literature. [1. Buses.] I. Title. II. Series.
HE5611.L27 2000
388.3′22—dc21   99-24249
                                                                                                      CIP

Editorial Credits
Karen L. Daas, editor; Timothy Halldin, cover designer and illustrator; Heather Kindseth,
    illustrator; Kimberly Danger, photo researcher

Photo Credits
Corbis, 12–13, 14, 16
David F. Clobes, 8 (inset)
James P. Rowan, 20
Photo Network, 8–9; Photo Network/Tom Campbell, cover
Photophile/Gary Conaughton, 4; Tom Tracy, 18
Unicorn Stock Photos/Tommy Dodson, 6

Table of Contents

Buses

Buses are large, motor-driven vehicles. Buses carry many passengers at one time. Many buses travel on city streets. Bus drivers follow routes. Drivers make many stops to let people on and off buses.

route
the path a vehicle or person takes
to get from one place to another

Traveling by Bus

People wait for buses at bus stops. A sign is on the front of the bus. The sign tells people where the bus is going. People pay a fare as they get on or off the bus. Passengers signal when they want to get off the bus. They push buttons or pull cords that ring a bell.

fare
the cost of traveling on a bus

fare
box

windows

driver

MONT

48 A

MONTEBELLO MUNICIPAL LINES

GARFIELD BANK

wheel

door

Parts of a Bus

All buses have the same main parts. A bus has wheels. A bus has many large windows. A bus has a front door. Many buses also have a middle door. The driver sits at the front of the bus. A fare box is inside the bus next to the driver.

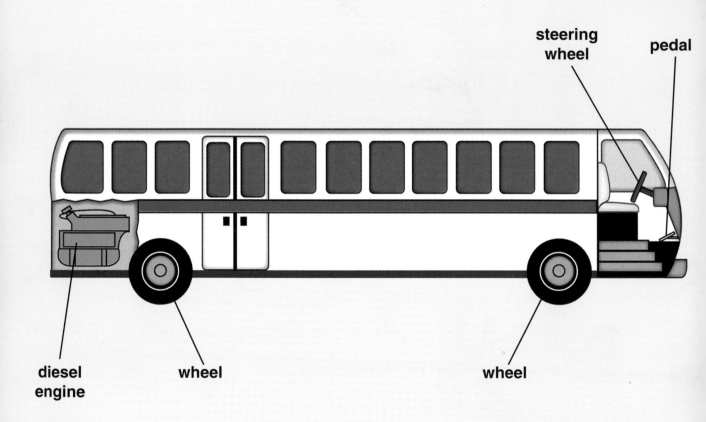

steering
wheel

pedal

diesel
engine

wheel

wheel

How a Bus Works

A bus driver flips a switch to start the bus engine. Most bus engines use diesel fuel to produce power. The power turns the bus wheels. The driver uses floor pedals to control the bus' speed and to stop the bus. The driver uses a steering wheel to control the direction of the bus.

diesel
a heavy fuel that
burns to make power

11

Before the Bus

People walked or rode in horse-drawn carriages before buses were invented. Carriages only hold a few people at one time. City streets became crowded with carriages. People began to look for new ways to travel within cities.

Inventor of the Bus

Blaise Pascal invented the bus in Paris, France. In 1662, he hitched a team of horses to a large wagon. He called his invention an omnibus. The omnibus could carry more people than any carriage could. Eight passengers could ride in the first omnibus.

Early Buses

In 1819, omnibus service started throughout New York City and Paris. Soon many people began to call the vehicles buses. Cities started using fuel-powered buses in the early 1900s. These buses moved faster than horse-drawn buses.

Buses around the World

Most countries have bus systems. Some countries use double-decker buses. These buses have two levels. Passengers can sit on the top level or on the bottom level. Some countries use articulated buses. These long buses look like two buses joined together.

Bus Facts

- Several countries in the world use trolley coaches. These vehicles look like buses. But they are powered by electric cables above streets.

- One early bus design had a large truck that pulled a trailer.

- The first buses in the United States carried only 12 passengers. Horses pulled these buses.

- People in U.S. cities ride buses more than any other form of public transportation.

- More than 4.5 billion passengers ride U.S. city buses each year.

- A passenger rides a city bus an average of 4 miles (6 kilometers) each trip.

Hands On: Maps

Buses follow routes. A bus route map will tell you which bus to take. On this map, each bus route is a different color. You can practice reading maps.

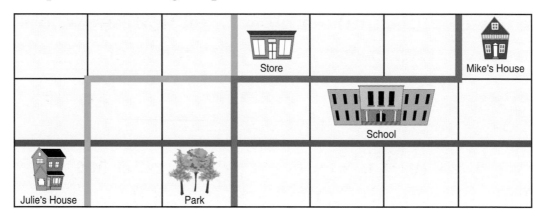

1. Find Julie's house on the map.
2. Find the school on the map.
3. Find the bus route that goes from Julie's house to the school. Which color route would you take?
4. Find the route to go from Julie's house to the store without changing buses.
5. Find the route to go from the park to Mike's house.

Words to Know

carriage (KA-rij)—a vehicle with wheels that is usually pulled by horses

diesel (DEE-zuhl)—a heavy fuel that burns to make power; many buses run on diesel.

engine (EN-juhn)—a machine that makes the power needed to move something

inventor (in-VENT-or)—a person who has an idea for something new and makes it

passenger (PASS-uhn-jur)—someone other than the driver who travels by bus or other form of transportation

vehicle (VEE-uh-kuhl)—something that carries people and goods from one place to another

Read More

Graham, Ian. *Transport: How it Works.* New York: Sterling Publishing Company, 1995.
Wilson, Anthony. *Visual Timelines of Transportation.* New York: DK Publishing, 1995.

Internet Sites

Bob's Bus Station
http://www.dot.gov/edu/k5/bus.htm
The Museum of Bus Transportation Slideshow
http://www.busmuseum.org/slides.html

Index